Samuel French Acting Edition

The New Black Fest's Hands Up
7 Playwrights, 7 Testaments

Superiority Fantasy
Nathan James

Holes In My Identity
Nathan Yungerberg

They Shootin! Or I Ain't Neva Scared...
Idris Goodwin

Dead of Night... The Execution of...
Nambi E. Kelley

Abortion
NSangou Njikam

Walking Next to Michael Brown
Eric Micha Holmes

How I Feel
Dennis A. Allen II

SAMUELFRENCH.COM   SAMUELFRENCH.CO.UK

FOR PRODUCTION ENQUIRIES

UNITED STATES AND CANADA
Info@SamuelFrench.com
1-866-598-8449

UNITED KINGDOM AND EUROPE
Plays@SamuelFrench.co.uk
020-7255-4302

Each title is subject to availability from Samuel French, depending upon country of performance. Please be aware that *HANDS UP: 7 PLAYWRIGHTS, 7 TESTAMENTS* may not be licensed by Samuel French in your territory. Professional and amateur producers should contact the nearest Samuel French office or licensing partner to verify availability.

No one shall make any changes in this title(s) for the purpose of production. No part of this book may be reproduced, stored in a retrieval system, or transmitted in any form, by any means, now known or yet to be invented, including mechanical, electronic, photocopying, recording, videotaping, or otherwise, without the prior written permission of the publisher. No one shall upload this title(s), or part of this title(s), to any social media websites.

For all enquiries regarding motion picture, television, and other media rights, please contact Samuel French.

MUSIC USE NOTE

Licensees are solely responsible for obtaining formal written permission from copyright owners to use copyrighted music in the performance of this play and are strongly cautioned to do so. If no such permission is obtained by the licensee, then the licensee must use only original music that the licensee owns and controls. Licensees are solely responsible and liable for all music clearances and shall indemnify the copyright owners of the play(s) and their licensing agent, Samuel French, against any costs, expenses, losses and liabilities arising from the use of music by licensees. Please contact the appropriate music licensing authority in your territory for the rights to any incidental music.

IMPORTANT BILLING AND CREDIT REQUIREMENTS

If you have obtained performance rights to this title, please refer to your licensing agreement for important billing and credit requirements.

HANDS UP: 7 PLAYWRIGHTS, 7 TESTAMENTS received its world premiere at Flashpoint Theatre Company at the University of the Arts on June 13, 2015, directed by Joanna Settle. The cast included: Aaron Bell, Lee Edward Colston II, EZ Hernandez, Johnnie Hobbs, Jr., Brandon J. Pierce, Brian Anthony Wilson, with live music by Ill Doots.

Philadelphia's Barrymore Awards: Outstanding Original Music: Ill Doots for *HANDS UP: 6 PLAYWRIGHTS, 6 TESTAMENTS* (Flashpoint Theatre Company).

HANDS UP was also a Philadelphia's Barrymore Awards nomination for Independence Foundation Award for Outstanding New Play.

HANDS UP: 7 PLAYWRIGHTS, 7 TESTAMENTS was originally presented as a staged reading at the Martin Segal Theatre at Cuny Graduate Center, New York City on November 14, 2015. Directed by Carl Cofield. The cast included: Eric Micha Holmes, NSangou Njikam, Jamie Lincoln Smith, Marcel Spears, Bjorn Dupaty, and Terrell Donnell Sledge.

HANDS UP: 7 PLAYWRIGHTS, 7 TESTAMENTS received a workshop production at the National Black Theatre in New York City on February 14, 2015. Directed by Jonathan McCrory. The cast included: Joshua Boone, Kamal Angelo Bolden, NSangou Njikam, Jahi Kearse, Jevon McFerrin, Chinaza Uche.

The New Black Fest was founded in 2010. Its mission is to fulfill a need among Black American and Diasporic playwrights for further opportunities to develop new work and, as advisory board member Lynn Nottage says, "sustain our complexity." The New Black Fest's agenda is both political and artistic: it encourages Black playwrights to strive for diverse aesthetics, perspectives, and subject matter. Keith Josef Adkins, Artistic Director and Co-Founder.

TABLE OF CONTENTS

Superiority Fantasy

Nathan James

CHARACTER

NATHAN – African American Man (Both parents identify as African American, with roots in American Slavery.)

(Man speaks.)

I think there is a difference between a Caucasian person, and a white person. A Caucasian person is one whose skin just happens to be lighter than yours. They are just trying to get through life in America just the same as black people are, and they don't treat you any different than anybody else. But a white person? When a white person walks into the room, you can tell by the way they look at you that they KNOW they're white and you're black. It's the smugness in their face when they look at you. They come to events in our community and act like they should have special treatment, or some merit badge for coming off their high horses and spending an evening with the help. And when you enter into majority white areas, they look at you like you're lost. What you are about to hear, will not be pleasant for your ears. When I speak of white America, I do not speak of every white citizen in America. I speak of the majority of America, who influence the laws that keep the good-ole-boy network in power, or reap the benefits of it, while giving their silent consent in order to protect their privilege. It's pretty much the same as I feel about cops. I know they're not all assholes. I know some who actually do a lot of good in the black community. If my loved ones, or I, were in danger, I would surely call them. But as for the majority of them, I hate cops! I wish that I could stand here and tell you something politically correct. I wish I could make my language nice and plentiful for your ears, but I wouldn't be true to myself if I stood here and told you that I trusted ANY cop that I didn't know personally before he put on that badge. Any time I see that uniform, I immediately begin to think about all the times those bastards have harassed me ever since I was fourteen years old.

A few months ago, I had just left the barbershop, and I was headed to the Urban World Film Festival. I knew there would be some pretty fancy events during the festival...so I knew I couldn't walk up in there looking basic. I hit up H&M for a new outfit. Hit up the barbershop up on 125th. I went in my closet and pulled out the "good shoes." I was FRESH! One of those days where you feel like you have the world at your fingertips. One of those days where you have unstoppable confidence. Even the ratchetivity that was destined to await me on a New York City subway couldn't fuck up my vibe, as Jay Z's "Beach is Better" blasted through my headphones. I walked down the steps to the subway at 207th Street, gliding down each step like I was walking in slow motion in a music video. Needless to say, I was feelin' myself that day. I hit the bottom of the steps, and I was immediately stopped in my tracks by the police table at the bottom. Three white officers and one black stood at a table with a sign that said "NYPD will be conducting random bag searches. All searches are random. We do not need your permission to search your property." My Adam's apple dropped into my stomach. The two white guys in front of me walked through the turnstyle with ease, but I froze. I thought back to when I was I was driving one night in Pittsburgh.

I pulled up to a stop sign behind a rustic-red Chevy that was literally going fifteen miles an hour, on a twenty mile an hour street. I stayed patient for two blocks. The shit got annoying so I went around him. After that, he began to speed up...getting really close to my bumper. Naturally, I sped up to get away from him. He began to speed up again, pulling up close to my bumper. You see...I was from Beltzhoover [Belts-hoover], and I was in Homewood. Even though both neighborhoods were Crip territory, it very well could have been Bloods looking to do a drive by. I decided to punch it and get the hell out of there. This car chased me for four blocks. I pulled up to an intersection and was surrounded by police squad cars. I had been followed by undercover cops (who never flashed their lights or put on a siren). A few of them yanked my car door open and pulled me to the ground. All of the other cops had their guns drawn on me. As they pulled me out of my car, I heard one of them repeatedly say, "Where the fuck were you going so fast. Get your black ass on the fucking ground." They slammed me on the ground, one of the officers put his foot on the back of my neck. Another officer put a gun to the back of my head and said "Move one inch and I'll blow your fucking head off." They began to search my car. I told them that I wasn't a criminal. I said, "I'm an actor and a teacher." One of the officers said "Bullshit!" I told them it was true, and if they looked one block down the street there would be a billboard with my picture on it advertising my one man show. I went into survival mode. I tried to convince them that I was "one of the good ones." They radioed to a squad car to check it out. The squad car radioed back and confirmed it. They helped me off the ground as the undercover officer said, "Sorry about that buddy." He informed me that a car that resembled mine had been stolen, and my car fit the description. It was pretty odd because at the time I was driving a 2003 Dodge Neon. Who the fuck in their right mind risks getting caught by stealing a Dodge Neon. As he gave me my license back, he left me with, what he thought, was sound advice, "Stay out of trouble," as if I needed to hear that.

After thinking back to that moment and several others that would follow, I snapped back into the present to the possibility of a possible police search ahead. I began to sweat. My heart was pounding in my chest. I just knew I was going to get searched. I knew Stop and Frisk was over, but I didn't trust them. Was I going to stand up for myself this time? Was I going to be a man? I decided to be smart, and "smile." Their eyes locked on me as I walked through the turnstyle. I got through without being stopped. I became at ease at the fact that I had made it through the possible police search unscathed. I sat across from the two white guys who passed the table before I did. They were laughing at a picture on one of their phones and hadn't even paid the police search any mind. Ironically, they both were wearing hooded sweatshirts, and I was dressed-to-impress. I'm tired of walking around egg shells, and trying to be less aggressive just to make white people feel more comfortable around me. I started to ask myself how I started this shit…this apologizing for the color of my skin. Why did I immediately know what to do in that situation? The non-threatening smile and walk was my default. I had done it before I even got a chance to think. Thinking back to childhood, I remember many moments when I was out with one of my friend's parents. Before we would walk into any toy store, we always got the same lecture, "Don't touch shit…don't ask for shit." My friend's mother would always end the lecture with a famous quote from parents in the black community, "Don't go up in here showing y'all's color." It was something that was imbedded into the men of my generation at a very young age.

When I was seventeen years old, I entered into a competition in Pittsburgh for young black men called "The Mister African American Competition." It was a chance to win $1000, feature articles in all of Pittsburgh's newspapers, and to meet a lot of cute girls in our sister pageant "Miss Black Teenage." Well I won and I remember it being some of the best years of my life. The only thing that I never liked about it was that they made us smile throughout the entire evening. They made us practice our smiles every Saturday leading up to the pageant. After a while, all the contestants' cheeks started shaking because of having to hold that smile. The reason we had to practice our smiles always stuck in the back of my head. They told us that we had to practice smiling, so it could be our default face in public as we walked down the street, and maybe people wouldn't be so sacred of us. By smiling, we could come off as non-threatening, and white women wouldn't be so scared to stand next to us on elevators.

I am tired of feeling like something grotesque. EVERY race of people have sociopaths who do horrible things, and I am tired of taking responsibility for the individual black men who chose to live like animals...while white boys are not being treated like they could potentially shoot up an elementary school with an AR-15. I don't give a damn whether white people believe these stories or not. These things happened! You can justify it however you like, but this shit doesn't happen to white men. And it is so annoying to sit on a job and hear people having things to say about something they know absolutely nothing about. People act like racism is some huge dragon that lives up in the Hills of the Deep South. Racism is just a fantasy of superiority. It's a bedtime story that America told its children over and over again and they forgot to tell them it was all a lie. It is a lie that America doesn't want to wake up from, because it's a lie that has become convenient.

And because white people have never experienced the lower end of the stick of racism, they can't fully recognize when it is and isn't happening...yet they have so much to say about whether or not it still exists. The victim blaming of unarmed black bodies shows that white people aren't really tired of racism. White people are tired of "talking" about racism. They want us to shut up about it. They want us to pretend like it's not happening. They want us to look at Barack Obama, Michael Jordan, and Oprah Winfrey and believe that everything is okay with us because those three made it...therefore...we should be able to as well. We've had a black president, so racism must be over.

Whether white America wants to acknowledge it or not... things are very lopsided in this country...and we are SICK OF IT! We've been "talking" for too long, and we keep getting the same excuses. If we keep ignoring race in this country, something bad is going to happen. If black people do not start getting treated as human beings, if the police do not start treating us with respect in our own communities, if we don't start receiving some justice at the hands of these brutal murders...our patience WILL run out...and it can possibly steer this country into another civil war.

I no longer believe in the justice system in this country. It's open season on black people, and if you are not pursuing your license to carry…you're gambling with your own life. If they refuse to change these gun laws, then we need to play by their rules. We must establish a way to defend our communities from anyone who threatens it…white or black. If the police will not protect us, then it is time for us to start protecting ourselves.

(Lights down.)

Holes In My Identity

Nathan Yungerberg

CHARACTERS

MAN – A light skinned black man (early forties)

SETTING

Bare stage

(The stage is dark except for a spot that is downstage center. A light skinned black **MAN** *[early forties] enters stage left and starts pacing back and forth in the spotlight. He is wearing jeans, a black t-shirt, and carrying a backpack.)*

So I was gonna go, and then I wasn't gonna go and then... well I decided to go, but I was... I was just gonna bring my camera and take pictures and listen.

(The **MAN** *removes a DSLR camera from his backpack.)*

It was a community discussion about Ferguson and the current state of black men in America, and I was... I was afraid it was just gonna turn into another us against them, black versus white, never ending argument. And I was also hesitant, because I didn't think I would have anything to share, cause I've got all these holes, holes in my identity, from the lack of black culture, black experiences, black role models, I've got all these holes.

(Pause.)

A friend of mine recently sent me this cartoon called "The Talk," on the left it showed a white kid with wide innocent eyes, whose dad was having a talk with him and there were cartoon speech bubbles of birds and bees floating above their heads. On the right there was an image of this little black boy with wide, fear filled eyes, having a talk with *his* dad and in the bubbles above *their* heads, was a gun and lady liberty... I got the birds and bees talk...from my *white* dad, never got the other one.

(Pause.)

(The stage lights come up and he walks downstage right of a chair.)

In my mind, I half expected the Ferguson discussion to be filled to the rafters, hot and humid with angry people screaming, fists raised, in a heated frenzy! But what I found was a diverse group of eight or ten people, sitting quietly in a circle of chairs. But still, I decided to fall back into the corner, and just take pictures.

> (*The* **MAN** *picks up his camera and starts shooting. Eventually he sits down, holds his camera in his lap, and nods and smiles politely at the people around him.*)

The energy was...calm, but like the calm before the storm calm. It kinda felt like we were waiting for something; people, passion, anger, answers...hope. A brief announcement was made, a welcome and invitation to use the space and the time to share *our* truth. After an agonizing moment of silence, it began. A woman near the front spoke with intensity and clarity, a restrained river of anger and pain flowing beneath every word. A woman near her, exploded, her frustration with society collected on the walls like beads of perspiration. A woman to my right talked about her fear for the lives of her unborn sons, and then she started to cry. This man to my left spoke about the fact that his master's degree and high ranking job served as a flimsy shield against racial profiling. And a young man to my right said that he felt that the media was the culprit, in consistently depicting negative images of black men in TV and in film. And then a woman...a *white* woman sitting straight ahead, I'm giving her a qualifier because she went out of her way to announce that she was Italian; she spoke about getting stopped and frisked at the airport several times...four to be exact.

She spoke about the intense humiliation as they rifled through her belongings; she talked about feeling like a criminal. She said on the fourth occasion she asked them why they singled her out. They told her that she fit a profile.

> (*Pause.*)

And then she said "*Everybody* gets singled out at least once in their life, it's *not* about race, we *all* go through it."

> (*The* **MAN** *puts his camera down and sits up straight.*)

(*Quickly.*) And then my voice leapt forth from my chest before I had a chance to grab it.

> (*The* **MAN** *leans forward.*)

(*Loudly.*) ARE YOU FUCKING SERIOUS?!

> (*The* **MAN** *covers his mouth and sits up.*)

(*To himself.*) Shit! Did *I* just say that?

> (*The* **MAN** *nods, gathers himself, and leans forward in his chair with confidence.*)

What we're talking about here is consistency, *repetitive* profiling... *Constant* harassment... *Consistency*! And what you're saying is so so dismissive!

> (*The* **MAN** *tilts his head to the left as if listening and then sits up straight.*)

She asked me to explain *how* she was being dismissive.

> (*The* **MAN** *leans forward again.*)

Because when you're talking about issues of race, you *can't* just say that we *all* go through the same thing...
(*Quietly.*) Because we don't.

> (*The* **MAN** *sits up and tilts his head again.*)

She said she was just trying to have an honest discussion about race, that she wasn't trying to dismiss anyone's experience.

> (*The* **MAN** *leans in again.*)

(*Quietly.*) Dismissal steps quietly.

> (*Pause.*)

I was adopted by white parents and raised in an all-white, middle-class community and outside of my never ending identity crisis, my early life experience as a black American was extremely safe, extremely protected and extremely dismissed. When I was a kid, maybe eight, which was around the time that my racial differences were really starting to fuck with my head, I would try so hard to articulate my feelings to my mom and dad, but they just didn't have the experience or understanding to support me. There was this incident at school, where a kid was reading from a history book about Africa and he mispronounced the River Niger, you know how that ended, and all the kids turned towards me and snickered and my spirit just melted all over the floor.

I went home that day crying and my parents responded with, "Oh they didn't mean to hurt you," "When I was a kid, I had goofy hair and the kids made fun of me too." And my all-time favorite "Color. Doesn't. Matter."

> *(The* **MAN** *snaps his fingers.)*

Dismissed!

> *(The* **MAN** *sits up and looks to his left.)*

A woman to my left angrily shouted that white people always want to dismiss what they can't see!

> *(The* **MAN** *turns to the right.)*

And then a man to my right said if profiling wasn't real then there are a whole lot of delusional black men wandering the streets.

> *(The* **MAN** *looks straight ahead.)*

And then a woman straight ahead said that there is not one black person in this room that has not experienced some kind of issue with racial profiling, it's an epidemic! And if you can't see that you're blind!

> *(The* **MAN** *contemplates something for an uncomfortable moment and then leans in slowly.)*

(Quietly.) I haven't.

> *(The* **MAN** *takes a deep breath.)*

(Cautiously.) I'm forty-three years old and I've never been stopped and frisked, I've never been accosted by the police, profiling has...not been part of my experience.

> *(The* **MAN** *looks down for a moment and gathers his thoughts.)*

I've been imagining lately how I would even react if I ever *was* stopped and frisked. What would that feel like as a forty-three-year-old black man who was raised with middle-class white privilege, how the hell would that end up? I've been having a lot of conversations about this lately, questioning black friends about their experiences with racial profiling. I even called my parents and asked them if I ever brought up any incidents, but their memory banks came up empty too. The more I read and watched what was going on in Ferguson, and in the rest of the country, I started to feel disconnected from my race because of my inability to relate to the experiences of other black men, and it kinda made me feel...like a fraud... I remember a few years ago, in Brooklyn, someone gave my partner a copy of *The Little Black Book,* it was a survival guide for black males in the U.S. He said some lady gave it to him because there were important things in it for him to know. He left it on the bookshelf and one afternoon, I picked it up, wondering what words of wisdom were waiting inside. What I found were critical rules for the black man; what to do when confronted by the police. I put it away, because I felt like it had nothing to do with me.

> *(Pause.)*

And that disturbed me, it really did. I was speaking with my therapist about all of this and she was shocked, not about my feelings necessarily, but about the critical pieces missing from my past.

As a black woman who had raised five black boys, she was worried about me, because as she observed, I'd been dodging the bullets of societal targeting all my life, and she was concerned that I wasn't prepared, that my parents had not prepared me. The image of dodging these bullets all my life really stuck in my mind.

(Pause.)

But can you dodge bullets that you can't even see?

(The MAN *pauses for a moment.)*

A few months ago, I was walking around the lake with my partner. He's bigger than me and darker than me and has an altogether polar opposite experience with race then I do. There was a white woman standing near us at a crosswalk, and when the light changed, she bolted and he immediately stated that she was trying to get away from him. I stopped for a moment and tried to process what he said because it wasn't what I saw at all. I asked him why he always thought white people were running from him and looking at him negatively. I said that maybe he should consider that the woman was just late for an appointment or running behind for work and that he had no proof that she ran because he was black. She may have been, she may not have been, but what was real were his feelings and he was angry and hurt because –

(Long pause.)

(The MAN *drops his head.)*

I dismissed *his* feelings.

(Pause.)

And you know what was really going on? I was upset, because from one black man to another, I couldn't understand what he was feeling, and I thought I should, and I felt those holes inside me, those gaping holes and I fell right inside one.

But the thing about holes is that you always know when you've fallen into one. So I dragged myself out and stopped at the side of the lake for a moment to breathe… and then I told him what I wished that my parents would have said to me on so many occasions when I was a child;

I told him that although I couldn't relate to what he was feeling, I *heard him* and I was sorry.

　　　(Long pause.)

Cause that's where the healing begins...that's where it begins.

End of Play

They Shootin! **or** *I Ain't Neva Scared…*

A Reverberation in 3 Parts

Idris Goodwin

CHARACTERS

IDRIS GOODWIN – Black, mid/late thirties, a writer, performer, educator

SETTING

Present day, liminal

Part One: Another Bird Brain Evening

I'm still awake, agitated under low lamp light, desperate
for something to put me to sleep

every book in the house is caffeinated
jittering with injustice
every book, dark skinned dynamite

I stumble upon a quirky essay on Alexander Graham Bell
but that ignites into a litany of names lynched and hung
from telegraph poles

of course, I can't look away

I flip pages gritting teeth
wishing I'd remembered to pick up
more graphic novels at the library, more cookbooks and
academic poetry

my synapses explode

I slam the book closed
click off the lamp

when I hear that noise I been telling myself doesn't exist
for the last half hour

this thump and bang
for the last half hour

trapped between two panes of glass, a bird with its wings
and bird brain banging itself

confused
it can see out both sides
but can't get free

I can't open the pane into the house
because then I got a pissed off
bird in my living room
so I go outside

it's after midnight
and chilly

I am wearing baggy sweats
unlaced boots,
a sweatshirt

I fumble with the window
the bird more frantic,
banging and
pecking and
flapping its wings against the glass

It's dark
and I am a hooded black man fucking around with
a window outside a white house in an floating ivory palace

a well meaning city of literature
this Iowa city, this university town
where I have been pulled over so many times I have a PHD
in talking to cops

I take my hoodie off, the night crisp air
is dark and so am I

thump and bang
pecking and flapping
terrified

fumbling my hands, trying to conceal the flathead
screwdriver

The more I try to free this animal
the more imprecise my fingers

when a car rolls by, I stop,
dart into the garage

my mind flutters
The image of tattered flags blowing
gently – swaying

I focus instead on the window
wedging it from the outside
like the imaginary home invaders I fear
the mob of white Iowans who suddenly
have a change of heart
who look to decorate their own telephone poles

a car rolls by
slow,
daring me to go back to the window
rusty,
face another day of hooded sweatshirts
and bloody headlines
thump and bang
against the glass

Part Two: A True Race Man

I'm at a high school somewhere in rural Iowa
Doing my spoken word thing

After my performance a young high schooler asks me:

Does it always have to be about race?

I'd love to say "absolutely not"

That I ignore the fact
that the middle aged lady in Kentucky who said colored people
mistook me for the other black
guy in the room

I wanna be eternally hopeful

the young high school student just asked me if it had to be about race and I really wanna say

"From hence forth I will stop cataloging the crimes of white people
stop writing about the dead and martyred for the sake of the children
and for their future"

But that's not what I'm going to say

I will say

"Yes.
None of this is theoretical
the skin is real

the skin is a passport
it can be revoked
stamped
expire

it can be broken
the skin is the body's largest organ
Young man, It's always about race because I helped create
a child
In a wilderness that devours black,

this wild that waits, right now
ready to tunnel through the air at skin shattering velocity

I am full of theories
and I see boogie men
But the thing is: they're real

so everyday I wake up ready, with curled fist
squeezing the life out of hope

Its about race because I am here at your all white school
To present my diverse perspective
Because your school paid me to do so
Because they were given a grant to promote such activity
Why? Why am I here today if not to talk to you about race"

And he will hear *my* question
he will think before he answers

And the grant his school received to bring me here today
Will have been money well spent

And I will leave
Rewriting everything I wish I'd said – differently

Part Three: They shootin'!

I am walking through the grass
Underneath an endless sky

There is not a building
Nor airplane
No Freeway or Gas station

There are no Human beings in sight

Just breeze
And the tall grass
And the clouds

It's beautiful
And I am walking though the scenery doesn't change

In the distance I begin to see these masses
they are large, dark and still
As I walk the focus tightens
But they're still a blur

More or less

And just a few steps before my eyes will adjust
And fully identify them

I hear the steel tracks receive kinetic rotation
A smoke billowing whistle

And I turn to see the train blow by
And I hear a voice scream the unintelligible
Then another and another

And then one after another after another
Rifles clutched in hands
peek out from every window

And I open my mouth to yell
And sounds emerge but it's not my native tongue
It is strange and different

The rifles speak their language
Hurling epitaphs prodding
the bodies to run and fall

I can hear the laughter from the train
The counting, and daring and betting to see how many
more
Than last time
counting up numbers with each shot
The bodies fall around me

The locomotive thinks it's shooting buffalo
But they're killing men for sport
To harm a community they want gone
Whose land they wish to demolish and lay more tracks
upon

But it's okay
I'm just dreaming
I have to be

Who else would leave such a mountain of flesh
Stockpile so many skulls
Who would take aim at defenseless mammals

Stain these blades of grass
Sin in the wide open
Underneath the gaze of the endless sky

Dead Of Night…
The Execution Of…

Nambi E. Kelley

CHARACTERS

NIKKI – late twenties/early thirties, a passionate and fiery young woman who goes after what she wants in life with a vulnerable side that is also her strength

SETTING

A confessional

*(**NIKKI**, in a confessional.)*

Making love to me was the equivalent of what? Phone sex? Less than twelve hours earlier, he hikes up my mini and hoists me up on the kitchen sink and, well…you know. And then we talk sweet everythings in each other's ears and he whispers real clear "I love you." And in joy we fall asleep. And it's good. Like all the problems, the deceit, the not listening, the blow ups are all history, past mystique. And we are back. In the pocket. In the nook. Back. And then. Morning comes. And as he's picking up his clothes. And not looking me in the eye. And as I roll over still in post-coital bliss and trying to pull him in to me one more 'gin before he starts his day he lays the sermon on me. "Last night was a mistake, I was drunk." And when I question what he means he says that making love to me was the equivalent of phone sex. And he leaves. I lay there for a moment. Minutes. Hours. Stunned in my nekedness. Pained in forgetfulness remembering that this is the dude I've come to know him as. I decide I'm going to give him a piece of my mind. I get to his apartment door. "Act!" I say in my head. Play the game. He answers the door and I am as pleasant as possible, smiling from ear to ear. He makes me spaghetti in a frying pan mixed with garlic and butter. We are peaceful. I eat it happily. Maybe I won't have to cuss him out for what he said today after all. Maybe we can be calm and civil and dare I say, loving? I ask him "Can we talk?" He says "No." "We need to talk." "It's always the same. You talk and talk and I listen and listen and then we fight." I insist. He resists. But I win. "After a year of being together, why would you say our love making is like phone sex?" "Because it's true." "How can that be true when you say you love me?" "I like you. A lot. But I don't have passion for you. You're a good fuck, though." "Limp dick bastard!", I scream. And…he slaps me. I reel, dazed. Then

kicks. I reel, this time fighting in my mind to stay calm.
I'm not going to let his ugly win. He wrestles me to the
ground, puts me in a sleeper hold so I can't breathe, wraps
his arms around my chest trying to squeeze the life out
of me. Then he says it. "Bitch." "Bitch." "Bitch." "Bitch."
"Bitch." I switch. His ugly becomes me. Slugs me. So I can
barely breathe me cuz I'm too busy fighting him biting
him for my dignity. Through his front door he pushes
me. Onto Addison Street we spill. Good old white boy
Wrigleyville. Still he slaps. Kicks. "Bitch." And no one steps
in. No one stops this white man. My white man. White
boyfriend sonavabastardman. From slapping/kicking/
Bitchcalling little BLACK me. Flashing lights. Sirens call.
Yes! Po-po. Five-o. From down on Halsted Street. Yes!
I will be rescued. Saved! "What's the problem, sir?" My
raving lunatic white boyfriend becomes suddenly cool.
"Well officer, blahdy blah blah blah blah blah blah blah
blahdy blahdy blah, etcetera etcetera etcetera blah blah..."
I couldn't hear a fucking word cuz I'm thinking, where
did that motherfucker go that was just beating the shit out
of me? The blahdy blahs stop and I wait patiently for the
officer to turn to me. Address me. Ask me what happened
Miss. But I wasn't in the club. Officer Snow never once
asked little BLACK me what was the problem ma'am. From
my white man's word Officer Snow and all his boys swoop
down on me like white on rice. My breathing becomes
shallow, quick, from the weight of these six, yes, six, white,
yes white, cops, I keep screaming, "I can't breathe! I can't
breathe! I can't breathe!" A cop shouts back "If you can't
breathe then how can you talk?" I panic harder. So much so
that even my white man boyfriend gets scared, tells/begs/
pleads with the cops... "Please sir. She has panic attacks,
please sir, she's got problems with an irregular heart.
Please, sir, tell your officers to get off her. She's only 115
pounds sir. Please sir, please." I'm thinking, where was his
empathy sympathy feeling me when he was doing the same
exact shit to me? Now he cares? Still even his pleas fall on
silent ears, the visual to these cops of this angry BLACK
woman on this must be innocent WHITE man clearly has

taken over. Cuffs cuff my wrists that are now tired and limp from distress. They take my 115 pound cuffed BLACK ass and throw me in the back of the squad car. I sit. Winded. Broken. Unclear of all that just happened. Another white cop comes within inches of my face as I am working my ass off to catch what little breath is left in me. He says, "You want to go home or go to jail?" I open my mouth to speak. Nothing comes out. He slams the car door on my opened mouth. Carts me off to holding. Down on Halsted Street. Where I am surrounded by more and more cops. "You sure are a cute little thing." They say. "I can't believe you hit a cop, bit a cop..." I scream "I didn't hit a cop! Didn't bite a cop! You're lying!" "Whoa! Watch that mouth you feisty little girl or I'll add that to this list." Another says, "You're just so damn cute." They repeat. "So damn cute." Sweat on my brow in the now I am afraid. Anything can happen. They could beat me. Rape me. Kill me... I choose my words carefully... "But officer," I say, calming myself, trying reason through whispered tears, "I didn't do anything. My guy beat the shit out of me and someone called the police and nobody asked me what happened. They just sat on top of me. Six, yes six, cops sat on top of me... I couldn't breathe. I just couldn't breathe." My poetry. My rhythm. Gone. They throw me back in holding and I keep insisting on my phone call. At last I finally get one. I didn't call my family, or a close girlfriend. I call My White Man because somewhere in me I know if need be they gonna listen to him before my Black daddy. I try to tell him that cops are eyeing me, looking at my breasts, the curve of my hips, my little shelf of an ass and didn't listen to a goddamn thing I'd said. He ignores my words, tells me he'll call my brother to come get me, and then hangs up the phone. Dial tone. No care. No concern. When the fuck will I ever learn? They return me to my holding cell. Later they throw me in the back of a paddy wagon. They take me to a woman's facility. There are women cops. I think we are sisters! I try to smile. Be nice. Be kind. You're not like these people, I hear in my head. You don't belong here. They take my fingerprints. Pose me for my mugshot.

I smile, cause why wouldn't I? I'm taking a damn picture for posterity. "You ain't cute, bitch." A lady cop says to me. "Wipe that fucking smile off your face," another says. I learn real quick that I have to jump hard. Play the animal they are already treating me as. Or I will get swallowed. "Empty your pockets." I comply with a snarl so they'll know not to fuck with me further. "Spread your legs." They go up in me, touching me, feeling the outside and inside of me for weaponry. For a while. A long while. The invasion ends. Wait, what just happened? They throw me in a cell. The other cellmates try to talk to me, "What's your name, girl?" "What you in for, girl?" "You quiet, you must be a fighter, girl." I say nothing. Even if I wanted to, I can't.

Hours go by. Hours I replay the words, the scenario, the event. I finally just tell myself to shut the fuck up. It's broke. But I can't fix it. Can't fix it, can't fix it... I fall asleep. A knocking on the cell door wakes me up. "Your brother's here, girlie. Get the fuck up." I get the fuck up. My brother takes me to his house. His wife draws me an epsom salt bath. Nobody says a word. They can't. They just give me what I need. At five a.m., I fall asleep.

Morning. Seven a.m. I can barely move despite the epsom. I go to work. I have to. Can't even put on my uniform without drawing attention to myself that I am hurt, bruised, immobile. I go to the change room. Lift my shirt. Softball sized bruises are coming in on my face, arms, back, legs where he'd slapped me and wrestled me and squeezed me, where they'd thrown me on the ground and sat on me. White oppression from every direction. My shoulder is scraped and bloody from the scuffle with the concrete as I writhed scrounging for air while they sat on top of me. I put on a jacket and a hat so no one can see this White Man White Cop induced mess or look in my eyes.

That night finally put the fear of God in me that that White Man could kill me. And so after that night. I never go back. Never look back. For three months. Couldn't eat. Got diarrhea anytime I got anywhere near the police station, which was only blocks from my apartment. Three

months later. I lose nearly twenty pounds. Am rail thin.
But I got my dignity. My life. I never look back.

Still something changes in me. Walking by the police
station on the way to the subway, I'd often catch glimpses
of the arresting officer, the one who told me I was so cute,
who leered at me and stared at my breasts and hips and
ass. Sometimes he would even smile at me. I was never sure
if he remembered me from that night, or if he was just so
used to smiling at women who he hoped were impressed by
his uniform. And then one day I am close enough that he
decides to speak. I hold my head high, like Coretta when
they shot Martin, like Betty when they killed Malcolm. And
he whispers, "You still scratchin' and bitin' cops?" And then
I get it. I understand more deeply than I ever understood
anything in my entire life. These cops are bitches. I keep
going through life assuming that everyone is beautiful and
good and wanting to do right by other people. I believe
that even in the harshest of circumstances. But maybe.
Just maybe. There is a such thing as ugly. That people are
evil. That people fall short of each other all the time and
it is the way things are and the way they are supposed to
be. That cop failing me makes me stronger. But it almost
makes me more afraid too. That maybe I don't need
nobody else. That I have to be ready to kill. I wanted those
cops to be something they were totally incapable of being
– protectors. Shit, I don't need them. No one can take
anything away from me. Their protection doesn't add to
my life, I can't let it take away from my life. They haven't
taken away from my body or my soul or my intellect or
my spirit or my God, nothing. And, I am lucky. All he did
was look at my hips, my breasts, my ass, he didn't touch
me, rape me, kill me. And then again to be in the space of
thinking of "at least he didn't" is a sickness too. But I am in
the "at least he didn't" club. 'Cuz at least I wasn't Shereese
Francis, four cops sat on her on a bed and unlike me, she
stopped breathing. At least I wasn't Rekia Boyd, shot in the
head for just standing next to a man holding a cell phone
a cop thought was a gun. At least I wasn't Miriam Carey,

shot to death for allegedly speeding away from a White House check point. At least. At least. At least.

Abortion

NSangou Njikam

CHARACTERS

AMEN – Thirty-three years old. African American. Smart. Lovable.

SETTING

An apartment. A table with one chair. A written letter. A pen. An evelope. A box.

TIME

October 1, 2014

AUTHOR'S NOTE

This piece is inspired by the events in Ferguson, Missouri…and by all the events in African history where we have been victims of injustice.

(At center stage we see a young man, around thirty-three years old, sitting at a small desk, writing. Next to him is a box, partially open though we cannot see what's inside. The young man smiles as he finishes writing. He places the piece of paper in an envelope. He stands from the desk and steps forward to recite what he has written.)

Dear Beautiful Soul…

(AMEN smiles.)

I first want to say that I love you and I think you're great. I really do. I don't know you yet, because technically you're not a person…not in the physical sense. In fact, you're not even conceived. You're just an idea. That's how my dad described where babies come from. I was about six years old and I looked up at him and said "Dad, where do babies come from?" He smiled and said "Amen, babies are ideas waiting to be born. They live in two parts. Half of the idea is with a man, and the other half with a woman. One day, when it's right, a man and a woman will come together and say you know, we both got good ideas, let's make one together. And not too long after that, the idea is born." I remember asking him "But Dad, not all ideas are good. Some are bad." He says, "No idea is good or bad when it's born. It's only how we raise it." I asked him "Was I a good idea? Am I a good idea so far?" "Yes, Amen, you are a wonderful idea."

(AMEN pauses for just a second…then…)

I figured I'd take the time now to talk to you, feed you with some love because you are a wonderful idea. You come from a long line of wonderful ideas and people who know how to make ideas grow. My parents sure did. Their parents did, too. Now understand, ideas take time. That's your first lesson. Ideas take time, and sometimes it ain't the right time for your idea. Ideas can be pretty scary at first, because you don't know what's gonna happen. I mean, think about birth. Every time a baby is born you're looking at a roll of the dice of life. And that can be scary. And imagine if your idea is a good idea. Imagine if your idea is something that could change the world. Sounds great, right? To some, but other people may not want the world to change. They may want it to stay just like it is because it works for them. Even if the world truly does need changing, you gotta know when to change it. Ideas take time.

(AMEN thinks, smiles, then continues.)

Lesson two: a smile is everything. Now, this is probably the corniest lesson I'm gonna give you, but yo, it's so true. Smiles are like hall passes in school, you have one and you can go anywhere. It's amazing. It's like a universal symbol of people saying "I'm just over here feeling good." You know what's funny? When you smile at somebody and they are too shy to smile back, but they kinda let a small smile out. I'm thinking "Now you know you wanna smile back. It's okay. Smile on the inside then. That's cool. At least you smiling, right?" If you just walking around smiling, the world opens up and gets a little easier. Because people know that you got something we all want. Now, this next lesson is serious. Very serious. When you are at a party, and they say "Throw your hands in the air, and wave them like they just don't care"…do that shit. Do that all the time. Your hands should go up, and stay there. Wave them around like you just don't care because in that moment, in that one tiny space of a moment, you will know what freedom feels like. And man, that is an addictive feeling. Eyes closed, hands making the air move and become wind, feet planted firmly in the spirit of not giving a fuck. That is freedom. And don't let nobody tell you otherwise. In fact, don't let nobody tell you NOTHING without you investigating it for yourself. See, the problem is people always saying that they know something, and don't really know. They'd rather sound smart than be smart. Smart is rough. People hate smart people. Hell, smart people hate other smart people because they can't be superior anymore. Smart is power, and the one thing fake power hates is real power. So be smart, even when it gets hard.

(**AMEN** *stops smiling.*)

And don't be afraid of hate. A lot of people talk about love but not about hate. I talk about balance. Thats what I believe. If you love God, you gotta hate the devil. If you love freedom, you gotta hate bondage. Hate, like love, is dependent upon the user. It's like…like a lightsaber. Some will use it for good. Those are the ones you hang with. The ones who use their feelings for a greater good, but how do you know? How do you know what's the greater good? I'm glad you asked. When life is affirmed. When life matters, you can use death to make sure life can go on. On earth, we call that sacrifice. It's honorable…sometimes. Other times it's stupid, but it's like I said, you gotta know how to handle your lightsaber. The only emotion I don't fuck with is fear. That one is like the bastard stepchild of emotions. You know the first thing I was afraid of? Those seventeen year cicadas. Every seventeen years, these little insects that have been living underground all this time suddenly bore holes from the earth and start flying around. Thousands of them. They come out for like three weeks or something, just to mate…mate and die. Ain't that crazy? They're big and they run into you and the sound they make while they're flying…you get no sleep. I didn't want to go outside. Dad says, "Son why are you so afraid? They not even thinking about you. You know what they're thinking about? Sex. All they wanna do is have sex. They've waited seventeen years for this moment. They're just teenagers, looking for a good time before they die. If they run into you, remember it was you that was in the way. You blocking their sex mission. They don't bite or scratch or attack. All they want is love. Now get on outside and play." I remember walking outside that day, seeing all those cicadas flying, and I thought to myself "They not thinking about me; they just want sex." And I stepped outside…and nothing happened. I was in the cicadas' world and they couldn't care less. And I was safe. I had always been safe, even if they were out to get me I am bigger and stronger than them. But they weren't out to get me. You know what blocked me? Fear. Somehow, whether it was through TV or movies or whatever, I had learned to be afraid of things that look different from me. Even if they ain't worried about me. Even if they just want sex.

(AMEN *gets serious.*)

Oh yeah...and sex...sex? Yo, sex is the most unfair thing ever. Sex is like Willy Wonka, just tempting you with chocolates and candies, knowing you want them. Who doesn't? And he's got something for everyone. You like fruit flavored candies? Sex has got them. Chocolate, or vanilla? Sex got that too. Shoot, if you like, sex can make you a chocolate vanilla swirl that'll blow your mind. And you'll be hooked. I'm a tell you right now... TAKE YOUR TIME when it comes to sex. Be like a cicada. Wait seventeen years before you go crazy. Sex is tricky. Like I lost my virginity, right..and I was thinking "Is this what everyone is so hyped about? This is why people lose they minds? Over this? I'll pass." Yeah, and then it hits. It's like someone flips a switch and sex becomes liquor. It just tastes better with every sip. And then...you're a wino. Losing your money and your mind over something that animals do in seasons or for reasons and you're a lifetime junky. I love sex. I feel like I could do it forever...but I won't. I haven't. It's consequences to that shit. I mean, sometimes a person look like they a good idea...but nope, they're not. Ideas, like books, gotta be judged by their content. You think you picking up a decent family tale, come to find out she's a graphic novel. Or you think she's a graphic novel and she turns out to be a murder mystery. Sounds crazy? Good. Remember that. Don't let your hormones take you off your game. Hormones, pheromones...nothing moans, you hear me! Leave the moans alone for a while. Sorry. Went a little far on that one.

(AMEN *eases up a bit.*)

It's about love. Love, man. That right there is complex. It means so many things to so many people, and most of us don't know how to do it, or how to do it right. If love was a lightsaber, we'd have to be Yoda to get it down pat. People say they know what it is. That's kinda true. I gotta admit, I don't know if I know fully what love is. I know bits and pieces of it. I do know that love and God are synonymous. The only thing you'll ever see is Love's backside, and that's if you're brave enough to peak when Love walks by. And I must admit, Love got the finest ass I ever seen. It don't make you want to just go and fuck her. It makes you want to... Be Her. Love makes you wanna lose yourself and just become formless. Love makes you want to go back to being an Idea. Unbounded, uncompromised...free. Love always wants to be free. Love and freedom have been going steady for a while. And if you want freedom, you have to love so fiercely that you would lose yourself...sacrifice...and hate not being in the presence of Love so much that you'd give anything...just to see that fine ass backside.

(**AMEN** *becomes somber, serious.*)

So um... I guess this is the part where I got to tell you why you'll never be born. At least not through me. I know, right? All this time telling you life lessons for a life you won't live. Messed up, I know, but not without reason. I've been thinking about you for a while now. Like for three or four years maybe. I thought about what it would be like to see you for the first time. To hold you. What it would be like to calm your cries. How I'd smile when you tried to speak, and applaud when you took your first steps. I thought about how much I'd protect you from every rock or stone, every uneven sidewalk or bee sting. How I'd be Daddy, big, strong, confident, loving, Heathcliff Huxtable Daddy...with a splash of James Evans, Sr. I thought about that...all of that...and I cried. My mom and dad, when they were younger, they worked their asses off to try and make the world a smooth place for me to be. They tried to make it easier, so I wouldn't have to go through what they had to endure. I wouldn't suffer or want for what they wanted. But what have I done? How have I made anything better? Let me tell you, if you came here, life would be no different than it would for me when I was coming up. Maybe the technology would be different. Maybe you wouldn't know about Saturday morning cartoons, landline phones with three-way, Star 69, or music videos, but the pain...the fear...it's still the same. I haven't done nothing. And I'm ashamed. How did I fuck up long before anybody ever gets the chance to call me Daddy? How can I bring you into a world I haven't made better? I mean, what kind of a father is that? I won't have it. I will not love you underground all this time, protecting you, shielding you from harmful lights and sounds, giving you all that I got, only to release you after seventeen years so you can fly and be killed while you was out just looking for sex and love...killed by some coward, gun-toting, uniform-wearing motherfucker who don't know that you wasn't even thinking about him...you just wanted to chase Love's backside. I will not have you become my cicada. I'm sorry, Dear Soul, but I can't bring you here. Not until I've done my part, and made the world different, better for you to be here.

> (**AMEN** *goes into a box, pulls out a vest lined with explosives, and puts it on.*)

I didn't tell anyone about this. Didn't tell them I planned to wear my funeral shroud under my jacket, walk down the street, smiling...with happy thoughts of you on my mind. Walk all the way down to the police precinct on Tompkins Avenue. Walk in with a smile and walk right up to the front desk and say "Excuse me officers, I have a great idea," and then... *(Quietly.)* Bang. They would all say "Hold up, this is a bad idea." Let me tell you one last thing about ideas. I'm sure I could've gone another way. I could do something less severe but... *(He thinks for a moment.)* if everybody worships and applauds sacrifice, if we all need someone to do what we're afraid to do...if we need someone to love so ferociously that they hate what might happen if we do nothing...well, I wanna be that sacrifice. That's how much I love you. And when I'm done, while all them blue badges are rotting in hell for what they've done, I'm gonna spend eternity chasing Love's backside. Well, I gotta go. I hope you understand. Maybe you should wait seventeen more years for things to change, but I promise you...this world will be different. I love you...so much. Sincerely, your would-have-been father...Amen.

> (**AMEN** *puts on a jacket over his vest, puts the letter in an envelope, seals it, then puts it on the desk. He looks out, smiles, gets serious and then... Blackout.*)

End of Play

Walking Next to Michael Brown

Confessions of a Light-Skinned Half-Breed

Eric Micha Holmes

CHARACTER

ERIC MICHA HOLMES – A man in his thirties with a White mother and Black father. He has dark hair, light eyes, and passes as White.

SETTING

A bare stage

TIME

Present

I

An Intervention

If I were walking next to Michael Brown on Canfield Drive in Ferguson Missouri, the day he was murdered by Officer Darren Wilson for stealing cigars, I would've said the magic words.

These seven words are passed down from White mothers to their sons. These are the seven words White people wish Black people would say. If Black people didn't trifle, if they weren't actually doing anything wrong, if they just said the magic words...then they wouldn't keep getting shot.

Fear not, Black people.

I know the magic words.

For I am half White.

Officer Wilson would be on one side; Michael Brown on the other. And I would stand in between. Hands up. In a gesture of bi-racial peace.

I turn to Officer Wilson who meets my eyes, green eyes I inherited from my Black grand daddy who died before we met, who never had the chance to tell me how proud he was, of me, at this moment. And then, just as the officer's finger wraps around the trigger, I say them:

"But, officer. There must've been a miscommunication."

Surprised, officer Wilson lowers his gun.

"Why thank you. Thank you, son, for your calm demeanor and respect for an officer of the law. May I see the receipt for your friends' cigars?"

And I'd say, "But of course. Mr. Brown? Would you care to show Officer Wilson the receipt for your cigars?" And Mr. Brown would say, "Behold, officer! Forsooth the receipt for my cigars." Wilson takes the receipt, inspects it – but not closely – hands it back.

(*British accent*)

"Well. Everything here looks in order. All's well and good then, boys. Tally-ho!" And we say:

"Tally-ho, Officah!"

"Tally-ho, boys!"

"Tally-ho! Officah!"

"Tally-ho! Tally-ho!"

We watch him, Officer Wilson, walk away into the fog, twirling his nightstick and whistling Frere Jacques. When he gets home his wife entreats, "Darren, dear, why were you late?" And Wilson says, "Shut your mouth is why I'm late!"

And then they make love.

Sweet love. The kind of love you see in sex education videos with foggy lenses. The kind of love most couples reserve for special occasions: like anniversaries, holidays, and making parole. But not Wilson and his wife. Oh no. *Every*day is Valentine's Day and when they kiss they kiss long and hard and when Mrs. Wilson climaxes she levitates three and a half feet off the bear skin rug and beams of light shoot through her eyes and fingers. And when she falls asleep she dreams of rainbows and doves and Lionel Richie songs.

Finished, Officer Wilson puts on a robe over his holster (which he never took off) and walks downstairs to his den, smokes a cigar, and writes a check to the United Negro College Fund.

All because I said the magic words:

"But, officer. There must've been a miscommunication"

Now it's your turn. Say it with me. Ready?

(Leads the audience)

"But, officer. There must've been a miscommunication"

II

An Interview

If Charlie Rose asked me to speak on the subject of Race and America (which would never happen but I like to fantasize about wearing a tweed jacket on PBS), I'd have to admit the truth: I've never said the magic words because no one's ever called the cops on me. Not even once.

Except *once.*

I'd tell Charlie Rose about that one time, when I was around the age of Michael Brown when he was murdered, when I was young and bored and drunk and I thought it would be good idea to break into a friend's apartment at two in the morning. I don't know when she called them. It must've been after I threw rocks at her window and before I scaled a tree next to her second floor balcony. When I entered her room I saw her, there, a Single White Female, in her nightgown, perched at the foot of her bed – holding a phone in one hand and a butcher's knife in the other.

If she stabbed me it wouldn't have been because I'm Black; she would've stabbed me because I was a fuckin' moron.

"Now let me ask you something, Chuck." That's how I'd say it. *Chuck.* Cuz at this point we're like. Totally BFF.

"Now let me ask you something, Chuck. Was it luck that kept me from going to jail? *Maybe.* But if it was luck, it wasn't the first time I was lucky. I've been pulled over, more than once, without an ID in a borrowed car and was let go. I've been caught sneaking into concerts, nightclubs, public buildings. I once put an Anarchy sticker on a cop car during an Iraq War protest. This was the same protest where I joined a drum circle in the middle of an intersection and the cops escorted, that's right, *escorted* us to the sidewalk. No arrests. No tear gas. No gun shots."

"My blackness is a failed wish. A recessive gene, unexpressed, buried deep inside me, which no one has ever taken seriously – even *me* – no matter how hard I tried to perfect my crossover or quote Public Enemy ten years after they were cool. Have I never been arrested because I look just like another Tall White Guy who keeps a tan in February?"

Chuck's smile encourages me to continue, so I continue.

"No. The reason I've never been arrested for the color of my skin is because my skin is White. I just happen to have a Black father."

"But sometimes I wonder if my appearance would have mattered had I grown up in Ferguson – a town that is seventy percent Black, unlike my neighborhood, which was five. Maybe walking through Black neighborhoods makes you Blacker. I mean, it's not like I'm *that* White. My lips are full and my hair kinks in humid air. So maybe, if I were walking next to Michael Brown on Canfield Drive, I would've rocked that St. Louis Cardinals cap to the side with a little less irony. Maybe I would've helped him steal those cigars because I wasn't in rehearsals because Normandy High, where Michael Brown graduated, had no theatre department. Maybe I would've spent more time at the gym, put on some weight. I would've been more suspicious, more observant, more defensive, resulting in a more persuasive swagger so that from a distance Officer Wilson, through his tinted windshield, would've seen Michael Brown walking next to Another Tall Black Dude wearing a red cap obscuring his green eyes."

"And maybe when Officer Wilson pulled up to the curb and grabbed Michael Brown by the throat, I would've run out of time."

"Because 'Officer, there must've been a miscommunication' takes about four seconds to say. Michael Brown was shot six times":

"Officer (bang!) there musta (bang!) been a (bang!) miscommuni (bang!) cation (bang! bang!)."

That's six shots in four seconds. Compare that to the following phrases. Each one, by itself, takes less than two:

"What the fuck?!"
"But I'm just goin' home!"
"What I do?!"
"Why you followin' me?!"
"I ain't do shit!"
"I said I'm goin' home!"
"I'm unarmed!"
"My hands are up!"
"I said I'm unarmed!"
"I can't breathe!"
"I can't breathe!"
"DON'T SHOOT!"
"DON'T SHOOT!"
"DON'T SHOOT!"

And then Charlie Rose says:
"Yes. Thank you. Now do it just like that when we're rolling."

III

No One Cares About Tragic Mulatto Problems

Dear Mr. Charlie Rose,

I'm writing in response to your most recent guest, Eric Micha Holmes, who shared his thoughts on Race and America yesterday in an effort to illuminate issues surrounding the recent spate of murders by the police in America. Mr. Holmes is my grandson. And as a Light-Skinned Half-Breed I'm afraid he could never, red hat on or off, be murdered because of his quote-unquote "Blackness." How can a bougie from the burbs contribute to a serious conversation about the crisis of the Black Male Body?

We're talking about a young man who, while living in New York City, was a twenty-five minute PATH train ride away from his Black family in East Orange and saw them a total of five times. That's five times in seven years. This is the same man who has the audacity to check "African-American" when he applied to the University of Iowa – that's right! – *Iowa.*Where he continues to peddle is soft-shoe "post-Blackness" on White academics who don't know any better. And let's not forget how many times he's let a White bigot use the word "nigger" in his presence without the slightest protest. How could he? How could he protest when deep down he knows that he can't speak for a group who he only visits five times in seven years – so he can collect a few bawdy antidotes for his next dinner party. "Leave the protesting to White Liberals," he thinks. "Let them with nothing to lose summon the bravery." And I'm sure it's with equal antipathy that he reacted to the news of Michael Brown because Black America is not my grandson's experience; it's his *material.*

Just look how often he visited his grandmother's apartment in Harlem to fill up on nostalgia for a time he was never a part of. And then he'd hail a cab downtown – back to the White world – a world where he has the freedom to go to a party in Brooklyn and choose, yes, *choose* when to drop hints of his inheritance when he thinks a pretty White girl will be charmed by the novelty of humping an octoroon.

Maybe this is a good place to point out that all of Mr. Holmes' girlfriends, much like his father's wives (the subject of my next letter,) were White. This isn't surprising. My grandson's mixed-race offers White girls the perfect opportunity to rebel without rebellion. He's punk rock without the Mohawk. How eagerly I can imagine his college girlfriend racing to the phone to call her mother. And after she tells Mommy that her new boyfriend is a Half-Breed, Mommy asks if she received the flannel pillowcases she ordered.

This change of subject is about the extent of my grandson's experience with racism. Racial profiling is not an issue of nuance. We're talking about what people *see*. We're talking about what an armed police officer *sees*, sometimes from a hundred yards away, in a moment of crisis. And this is a police officer who is trained and paid to assume the worst-case scenario and to act quickly. Officer Wilson did not murder Michael Brown after a long and rigorous exchange about the philosophical complexity of Race and America.

No.

He saw Black.

He shot Black.

Sincerely,

Luther Holmes

IV

Later That Night

After Officer Wilson wrote his check to the United Negro College Fund he took off his robe and got dressed for the night shift. At 2:17 a.m. he was dispatched to a Single White Female's address. She called 9-1-1 reporting a Young Black Male, probably drunk, throwing stones at her window before scaling a tree next to her second floor balcony.

And that's when she grabbed a butcher knife.

Fortunately, the Single White Female recognized the green eyes of Light-Skinned Half-Breed and screamed "What the fuck's the matter with you! You scared the shit out of me, dude! It's two in the morning! It's dark outside! I called the cops!"

And before the Light-Skinned Half-Breed could say "sorry" the front door kicked open. "But, officer, there musta been a –"

End Of Play

How I Feel

Dennis A. Allen II

CHARACTER

Black; Male; age twenty and up

TIME

Present

(Enters; takes a moment to "take in" the audience.)

I'd like to start with a showing of solidarity. If you would please raise your arms straight up in the air. Everyone. Everybody please. Hold them up just like this. Keep them up. Now we're going to do a call and response. I'm going to say, "Hands up" and you respond with, "Don't shoot!" So when I say, "Hands up!" you all say, "Don't shoot!"

Hands up. Hands up. Hands up! Hands up. Hands up! Hands up!

I'd like you ALL to keep your hands up with me. Some of you won't, but try. I'm asking you to be uncomfortable with me for a moment, for this moment in time let's attempt to experience the same experience together.

A few days into the protests in Ferguson; I was at my girlfriend's apartment, lying on her bed, watching the news coverage and following the Twitter updates. We both had been following the events closely for the past few days on almost a 24/7 vigilance and the room was filled to the ceiling with our angst and anger, fear and depression; so we decided to take a break. Turn off the television and go offline. We sat silently for a second and then she turned to me and said, "Baby we've never talked about how to handle if we're out together and the police harass you. Like what do you think I should do?"

(A moment.)

I'm looking at a woman I love, a woman for whom as cliché as it sounds, I would literally give my life. I look at her and I see and feel her fear and it is a fear that I am all too familiar with; it is a fear that I was introduced to at the very moment of my conception. Surrounded by it for nine months and nurtured and loved unconditionally by it my entire life. This fear is all too familiar.

My mother has shared with me on a couple of occasions that when she was pregnant with me she would find herself praying that I wouldn't be a boy. Each time she admits this she cries tears heavy with the burden of guilt that only a mother can fully comprehend. She cries tears filled with a helplessness and anger that only someone born into a world that doesn't value Black life can truly know. She said, "I prayed that you wouldn't be a boy because I knew that from the time you were born, you'd be born with a bull's-eye on your back." This fear is all too familiar.

So when I look at my girlfriend and she asks what's the best strategy to keep me safe from police, from keeping them from violating my rights; keep them from injuring and possibly killing another unarmed citizen – because that's what I would be. I don't carry any weapons, never broke any jail worthy laws, but I am obviously Black and THAT has been reason enough to kill me for hundreds of years now.

(A moment.)

I'm not interested in giving you a history lesson, there are scholars out there way more knowledgeable than I am; don't want to talk politics or sociology; economics or psychology, again there are social justice professionals, activists and doctors that have given lecture after lecture, have written book after book, blog after blog – tons of information out there that can help you contextualize this world we live in. Google it. I want to share how I feel.

I think about Mike Brown. I think about him being shot to death and then left in the street for four point five hours, uncovered for the entire neighborhood to see. I think about the countless other names – the ones we know and the ones undocumented – beaten, tased, violated, shot, murdered at the hands of our so-called servers and protectors. I think about my girlfriend and my mother worried night after night – hoping and praying that when I go out I come home because they know I'm the prey and it's open season out there. Love and worry seem to always go hand in hand but it is a very specific "worry," the fear that comes with knowing that you're not protected by those that are hired to protect you – not only that but they are targeting you and it's illegal to protect yourself against those hired to protect you.

So how I feel.

Fuck you is how I feel. I know that's not a very sophisticated or in depth response but, Fuck you. I'll write something eloquent for another play. I wanted to write some inspirational, soul shaking, "I done seen the mountaintop," type monologue. Something that could heal the four hundred years of untreated trauma; cure us from the disease of white supremacy; humanize us in a way that we've never been humanized before. But, Fuck you, is all I could come up with. Your shoulders are probably burning a bit, feeling fatigued. Keep them up for me.

There are some people, of all races, colors and creeds, that believe that it is MY responsibility through "proper living" to combat white supremacist thinking. Some that use the terms, post-racial and color blind as if they were real things. Since we're on this magical mystical fantasy ride let's imagine together. Imagine a world where every single Black or Brown American only wore their Sunday best; all prayed to a Christian god; never said a cuss word; didn't do any drugs – not even prescription; and broke no laws. Never engaged in any violence whatsoever, unless of course they were being good patriots and killing Black and Brown people in some other country. All worked and never got on public assistance, no matter what the state of the job market or economy was; every Black person was married if they had children and were 100% faithfully monogamous. All graduated high school regardless of the poor school funding and poor living conditions and at the very least had a bachelor's degree and was never in debt. Imagine if Black people were morally, spiritually and financially better than any and every White person that has ever walked the earth. Perfect. Better than any human being has ever been.

Then and only then could we rid our society of institutionalized racism; prejudice and bigotry in America. Then and only then will White people see us as valuable human beings. Then and only then will we be able to see ourselves as valuable human beings. Imagine this world. What if I told you if you could just keep your hands up high we could create this Utopia together. But you can never drop your hands. Hands up! For the sake of Black people here in America and abroad keep your hands up!

No one can do it. No human can keep his or her hands up forever and this bullshit fantasy isn't the answer either. I am human. My life is valuable and I shouldn't have to keep my hands held high to prove it and time and time again keeping our hands held high hasn't gotten us treated like human beings should be treated. So how do I feel? Fuck you is how I feel.

I will not allow you to take away my humanity. Every time you tell me not to be angry. That I'm, "too aggressive"; that I shouldn't be out at night; that I shouldn't wear a hoodie and that I need to pull up my pants and when I comply to your orders and reach for my wallet you kill me anyway. When I drop to the ground and allow you to hand cuff me you shoot me anyway. When you put me in the back of the paddy wagon you break my neck anyway! Fuck You. Fuck you for coming into our neighborhoods telling us that our "no snitching" culture is stopping justice from being done, stopping you from keeping us safe but then turn around and subscribe to the exact same No Snitching policy within the precinct. Mike Brown was shot six times and he had NO WEAPON. His brains were blown out in broad daylight. His blood all over the concrete and was left there in the street uncovered for over four fucking hours there is not language strong enough to convey what the fuck I feel about that. Fuck you for not feeling what I feel. Fuck you for shutting down because I'm using "strong" language. I'm not safe, my father's not safe, my brothers and sisters, my mother is not safe because none of you value our lives. Police don't. Whites don't. Blacks don't. But I will not allow you to take away my rights, my humanity.

You indiscriminately killing me is a display of your power. Me giving zero fucks if you kill me is an exercise of mine. Hands up!

Hands up. Hands up. Hands up. Hands up. Hands up!

(A moment.)

(Actor looks at the audience, then puts his hands down.)

End of Play